ISBN 978-0-692-59324-0

This book is dedicated to my niece, Tori, and to her becoming a big sister.

I found out I was going to be a big sister today!

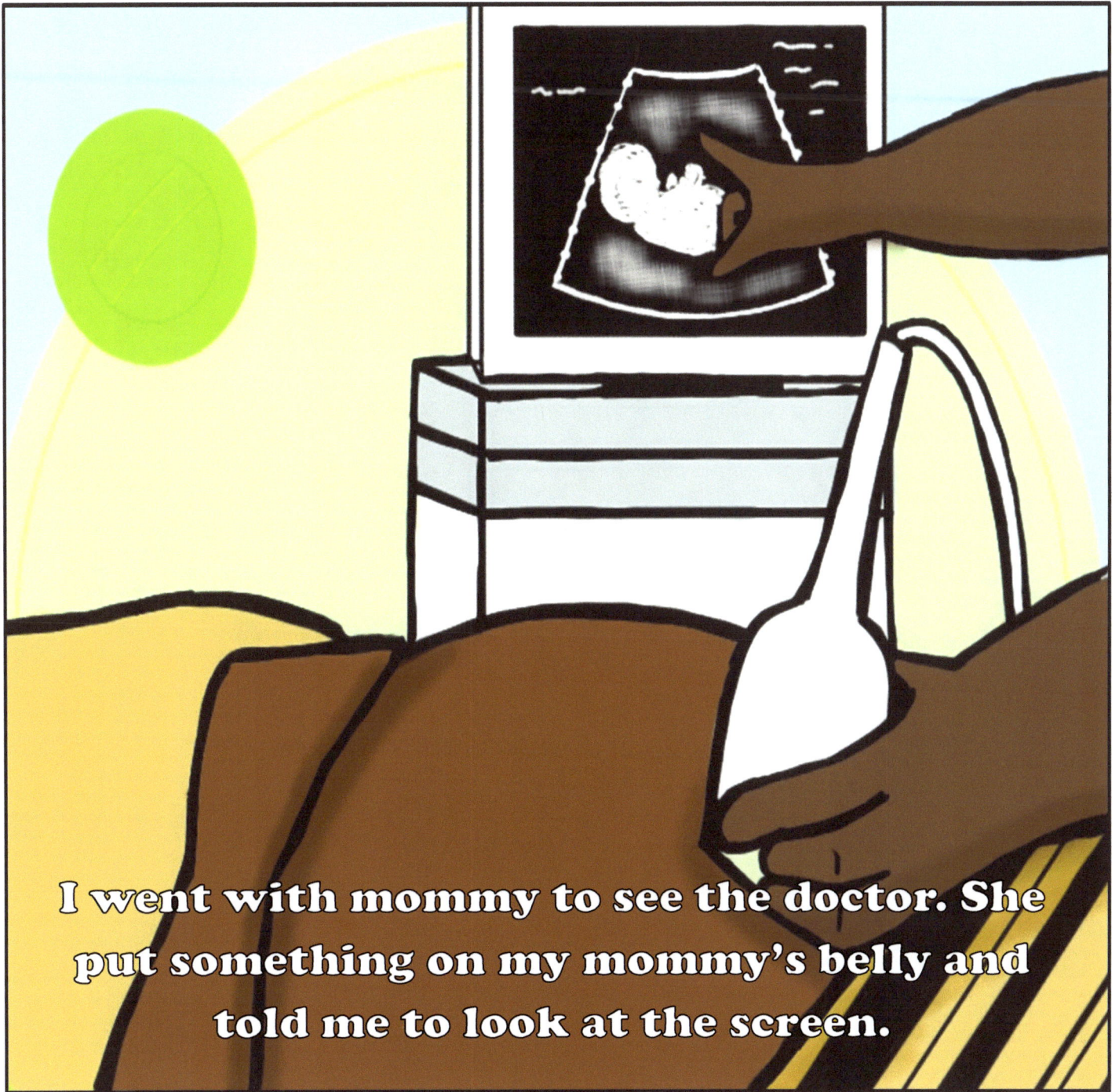

I went with mommy to see the doctor. She put something on my mommy's belly and told me to look at the screen.

There was a little thing moving around. My mommy said it was a sonogram of the new baby and that I was going to be a big sister.

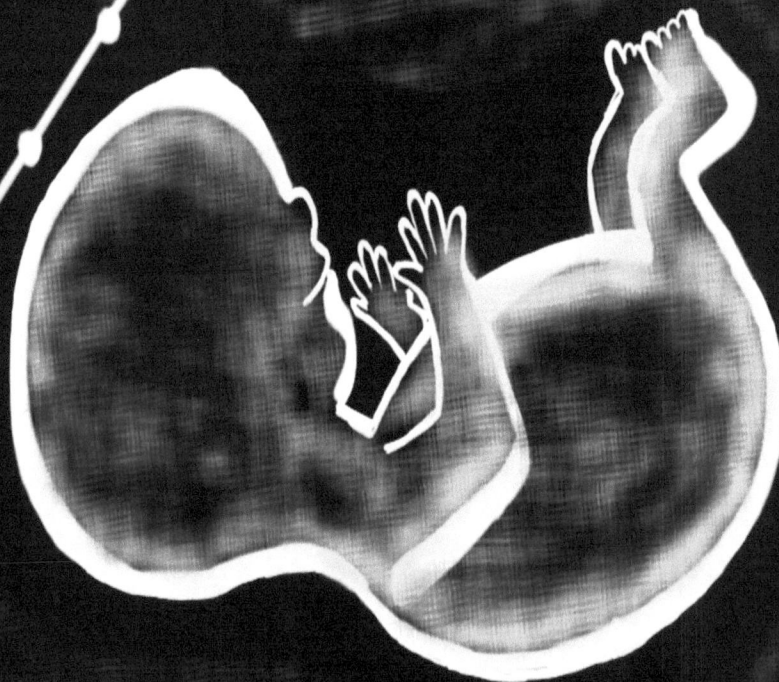

BABY A

01 : 27
0137
7033

HMI

Little me...
a big sister!

My mommy and daddy asked me if I wanted a little sister or a little brother.

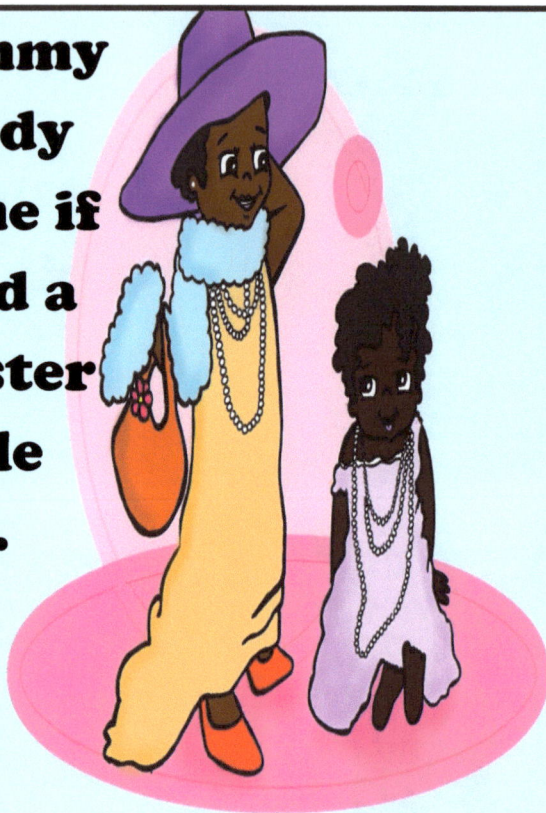

If it's a girl, we can play dress up together.

If it's a boy, I can chase him around the house.

A new baby means that I'll have to share everything, including my mommy and daddy.

Will they still love me when they have a new baby?

Mommy and Daddy said that they have hearts so big that they can love me and the new baby exactly the same.

They said they love each other, me, and the rest of the family, and they have plenty more room to give more love.

I believe them.

That means that my heart is big enough to love the new baby too!

Daddy says I will need to help mommy out with the new baby.

If the baby needs to be changed, I can get the pampers and hand them to mommy.

I can do things like put the pacifier in the baby's mouth when the baby cries.

I can even shake the rattle to keep the baby happy.

I'm going to be the best big sister ever!

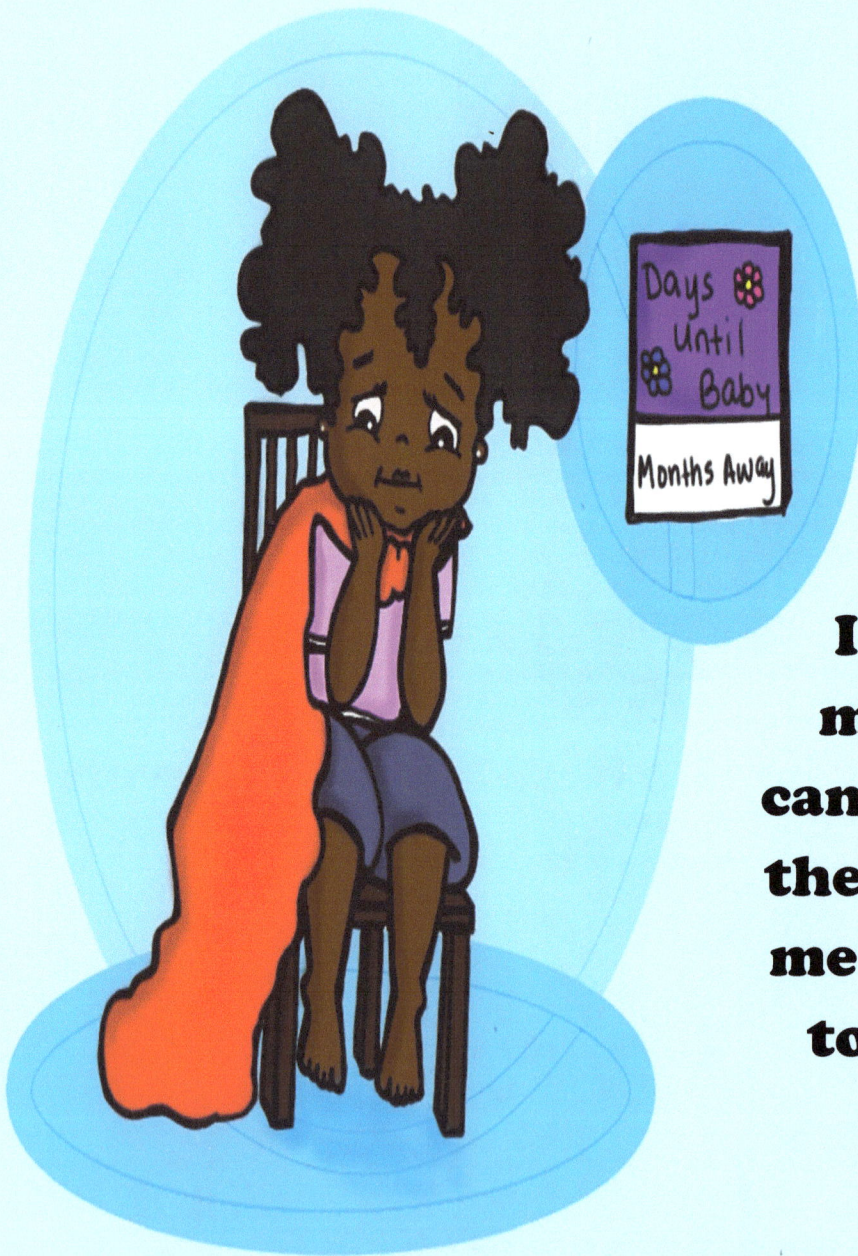

I keep telling mommy that I can't wait to meet the baby. She told me that I'm going to have to wait awhile.

Auntee says the
baby is growing inside
my mommy's belly,
growing each day
to get big enough to
be born so that we
can meet.

Big Girl Height

Grandma says that I am a big girl and that's why I am ready to be a big sister. I can't wait!

I'll be the best big sister ever!

Are you having a little brother or a little sister?

Thank you to my mom for the idea and my sister for the inspiration.

Special thanks to my youngest sister and her amazing talent in illustrating this book.

www.ingramcontent.com/pod-product-compliance
Lightning Source LLC
LaVergne TN
LVHW072110070426
835509LV00002B/106